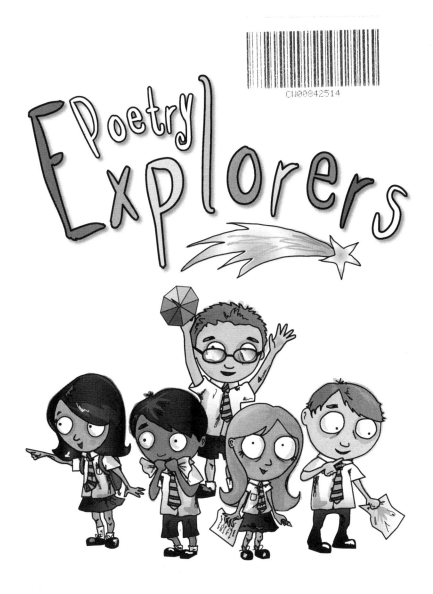

Heart Of England Poets

Edited by Lisa Adlam

First published in Great Britain in 2009 by

 Young**Writers**

Remus House
Coltsfoot Drive
Peterborough
PE2 9JX
Telephone: 01733 890066
Website: www.youngwriters.co.uk

Foreword

At Young Writers our defining aim is to promote an enjoyment of reading and writing amongst children and young adults. By giving aspiring poets the opportunity to see their work in print, their love of the written word as well as confidence in their own abilities has the chance to blossom.

Our latest competition Poetry Explorers was designed to introduce primary school children to the wonders of creative expression. They were given free reign to write on any theme and in any style, thus encouraging them to use and explore a variety of different poetic forms.

We are proud to present the resulting collection of regional anthologies which are an excellent showcase of young writing talent. With such a diverse range of entries received, the selection process was difficult yet very rewarding. From comical rhymes to poignant verses, there is plenty to entertain and inspire within these pages. We hope you agree that this collection bursting with imagination is one to treasure.

Contents

Webheath First School, Redditch

Wyvern Primary School, Leicester

The Poems

My Family

My mum is nice
She likes orange and ice.

My nana is the best
Better than the rest.

My sister is crazy
And she is lazy.

My dad is smelly
And he watches lots of telly.

My uncle Steven
Went to Cleven.

My auntie Kelly
Scratches her belly.

My brother is called Harry
He is too young to marry.

My brother
Has a lover.

My auntie Dee
Loves me.

My auntie Tracy
Has a friend called Stacy.

My cousin Briton
Only wears one mitten.

Rhia Tomkins (9)
Badsey First School, Evesham

The Panther

Deep in the jungle amongst the leaves,
A big black panther weaves.
Its eyes are emerald,
Its paws are big,
And it carefully steps on fallen twigs.

It spots its prey amongst the trees,
It stops and waits to seize,
Thinking about when to strike,
It skillfully prepares to pounce,
The prey is caught in one big bounce.

Its stomach full from the prey it took,
The panther drinks from a narrow brook.
To the trees it looks for shade,
So up the trunk it swiftly leaps
And with the day over, the panther sleeps.

Joshua Hartland (9)
Badsey First School, Evesham

Space

This is a poem, it's all about space,
If you look at the moon you might see a face.
There are lots of planets like Saturn and Mars,
They all live up there among the stars.
Lots of men have been on the moon,
They go in a rocket to get there soon.

Joseph Keyte (10)
Badsey First School, Evesham

The Blitz

I heard the air raid siren,
I went to tell my mum,
She said, 'Go get your brother, quick, come, come.'

Mum said, 'Go in the shelter,
But don't forget your mits,
It's really, really cold in there.'
I was shivering to bits.

The bombing soon had stopped,
And we all went outside,
The fires were all still burning,
My brother, well he just cried!

Jasmine Lymn (8)
Badsey First School, Evesham

Emma The Elephant

Emma the elephant was large and round,
With a tummy so fat it touched the ground,
She wobbled along with no speed at all,
And crashed straight into a rather big wall.

It crumpled and crunched and spread dust everywhere,
But she carried on walking like she didn't care,
Her long, curly trunk waved to all passers-by,
Then wrapped round her baby and lifted her high.

Sophie Metcalfe (9)
Badsey First School, Evesham

Nanny

I like it when Nanny comes to stay,
Because then we can play, play, play,
But when she doesn't feel very well,
I give her a spell, spell, spell.

I go 'Abracadabra cadoo,'
To take away her flu,
'Abracadabra cadee,'
Now she's happy with me!

Georgina Dare (8)
Badsey First School, Evesham

Haiku Poems

Underground Insect

Underground insect,
Digging through the moist, damp soil,
Wanting to be free.

The Sky

The sky far up there,
With the blueness of the sea,
Looking down at me.

Storms

The dangerous storms
Striking down at us humans
Destroying our homes.

Storm Adams (9)
Cosby Primary School, Cosby

Untitled

Sun,
Hot, warm,
Boiling, glowing, roasting,
Star, light,
Blazing.

Moon,
Dark, black,
Rotating, spinning, reflecting,
Star, light,
Planet.

Water,
Deep, blue,
Swimming, jumping, swaying,
Shadow, shallow,
Sea.

Volcano,
Hot, warm,
Boiling, erupting, glowing,
Star, light,
Blazing.

Waterfall,
Cold, fall,
Pouring, soaking, dripping,
Pond, puddle,
Freezing.

Drew Harbidge (8)
Cosby Primary School, Cosby

Kennings

Furry eater
Walking predator
Beastly mane
Three-clawed paws

Sleep lover
Plant eater
Easy snack,
Camouflage master

Head smasher
Water speeder
Giant monster
Farm habitat
Cart puller

Water sucker
Cart lifter
Vegetable monster
Giant flapping ears.

Krishen Chohan (9)
Cosby Primary School, Cosby

Dolphin

Grey as a rain cloud
Squeaky like a mouse
Beady eyes. Massive fins
The intelligent dolphin lives
Under the deep blue sea,

Finlay Lacey (7)
Cosby Primary School, Cosby

Untitled

Moon

Funfair
Bright light
Night-time
Hanging on a branch
Blowing

Sea

Blue, wide,
Fast flowing, salty
Underground
Atlantic

Candles

Wax, hot
Burning, smoking, smelling
Lead drifting
Light.

Michaela Christodoulou (8)
Cosby Primary School, Cosby

Dolphin

Cute, clever, cuddly dolphin
Swims under the deep blue sea.
The intelligent dolphin swims under the dark blue ocean.
Jumpy dolphin diving all day,
Swimming, splashing, squeaking, *'Hey!'*
Grey-white beady eyes pop squeaky, saying, 'Hi!'

Hannah Lacey (7)
Cosby Primary School, Cosby

The Sword And The Stone

No belief
But honesty
Blade as cold as ice
From minute to gigantic
Pulling and pulling
Only one could survive
Amazement shone
Upon faces
No belief
But honesty
Crowds marching
Like a herd of elephants
No belief
But honesty.

Tabitha Sullivan (10)

Cosby Primary School, Cosby

The Waterfall

Like a crashing avalanche the water fell to
its last destination.
The water was a raging bull charging
to its prey.
It jumped down to the shores like a kangaroo.
Splash!
The water fell like hail from the night sky.
It sparkled like diamonds.
It was soldiers running into battle to conquer
the shores below.

Elliot Spence (10)

Cosby Primary School, Cosby

Waterfall

As quiet as a whisper of wind
The flow of azure ran down the river
It twirled along the rigid path
Following its every twist and turn
Then it reached the end
Peacefulness and tranquillity was broken
The real journey had just begun . . .
Water abruptly fell from the peaceful heights above
Crashing into rocks on its way
It jumped between either side of the waterfall

Splash!

Finally plummeting into the depths of the mysterious pool below.

Lara Penn (10)
Cosby Primary School, Cosby

Waterfall

Stomping down the invincible rocks,
The water crashes and smashes.
The bombing water rampages,
Stopping for nothing at all,
As if it's a lion chasing its prey,
And springing like a man on a pogo stick.
The raging bull is the waterfall,
Going on in unstoppable rage,
Not stopping,
But plunging,
Plunging into its murky depths.

Matthew Breward (10)
Cosby Primary School, Cosby

Volcanoes

Volcanoes crashing everywhere
Leaping lava in the air
Spinning stars crash and fall
Vizard land blazing tall
Volcanoes explode like washing machines
When they bang, they get mean

Volcanoes wallop, volcanoes fizz
Volcanoes quickly, weirdly whizz

Volcanoes bang, sawdust and smoke
Like a rocket. Fizzing like Coke
The volcanoes have boiling steam
Working wonderfully as a team!

Freya Patten (8)
Cosby Primary School, Cosby

The River Poem

The water runs down the river crashing
into the rocks,
As the water is crashing into the rocks,
it slowly flows down off them,
With the water pattering down,
the river awakes,
Silent as a mouse, the water wriggles
down the river,
As the water charges down the river
there is a splash!

Tom Fura (11)
Cosby Primary School, Cosby

Water

The water swiftly runs down the snake-like riverbed
Resounding through the trees, the gushing river splashes
on the rocks
Swerving around the edge of the river
Rippling river meets the fish's destination
Gentle water is a graceful swan
Astonishing piles of blue jewels
The magical water cascades down the river
The river is like fairies dancing in the air
Silently, swishing, swiftly the river goes.

Ike Gill (10)
Cosby Primary School, Cosby

Waterfall

Gush, splash, splosh,
Plopping down to the target where the fishes play,
As loud as thunder,
Like marching soldiers,
Tumbling over each other,
Leaping over vast boulders,
Dashing aggressively,
Fearlessly, frantically, furiously gushing down
To the riverbed.
The destructive water is crashing like a bull.

Georgia Courtney (11)
Cosby Primary School, Cosby

The Sea Poem

As the sea slowly wakes up in the
gleaming glistening sunlight,
the dolphins amazingly jump,

Dancing merrily the gentle water
makes its way towards the mighty
rigid rocks,

Suddenly the sea turns into a mighty
whirlpool spinning like a ferocious
washing machine.

Erin Coleman (10)
Cosby Primary School, Cosby

Water

Like a crescendo of fury the water dances
down the furious river,

Glittering peacefully, the water is a gymnast
stretching from one area to another,

The water is like a blue ribbon rippling,
glistening down the rocky river,

A blue dress fitting perfectly around
the water's edge.

Madelaine Playle (11)
Cosby Primary School, Cosby

The Waterfall

The waterfall sparkled and foamed, but then it raged,
as quick as a blink it went mad and utterly harmful.
Its rocky slopes crumbled and plummeted down
and sank into a watery pit of destruction.
It ran down the slopes like an aggressive tiger
that left a trail of watery saliva behind its explosive bang.
It was a giant exploding with power,
knocking everything out of its path.
The waterfall.

Drew Green (11)

Cosby Primary School, Cosby

Waterfall

Weaving in and out, the water slid between the rocks,
Like a snake slithering cautiously,
Water charging, leaping, plummeting,
Crashing . . . tranquil,
Like a belly dancer trying to be irresistible,
Spraying, splashing water,
Roaring crashes, amazing crashes, terrifying crashes,
The water was a tiger leaping from rock to rock,
The water travelled.

Daniel Briers (10)

Cosby Primary School, Cosby

Streams

The water dived into a misty pool of adventure,
Spilling downwards at a rapid pace.
Sprinting like the Terminator, on a never-ending journey
Down the river,
As it raged down the waters like an angry bull
Destroying everything in its path,
Smashing into rock on the way.
Crashing like an avalanche into eternity.
Glittering with a beautiful blue aurora.

Jeremy Wain (11)
Cosby Primary School, Cosby

The Sword In The Stone

Sword is as still as stone,
Patterns red, yellow and green,
Shine sparkles in the moonlight,
Stone as big as a tree,
Sword as heavy as a castle,
Stone bold and strong,
Stone cold like a lake in winter,
Boy is weak but has a great future,
Sword swings back and forth.

Dominic Townsend (10)
Cosby Primary School, Cosby

Water

Like a raging bull the water finally reaches the dark,
murky puddle below.
The water crashes and smashes against the rocks
but nothing will stop it.
Falling from above, it is like rain falling from the sky.
Making sure nothing is in its way, the water plummets
from the top of the waterfall.
The water is like a light blue puddle surrounding the world.

Laura Bethell (11)

Cosby Primary School, Cosby

Flowers

Funny flowers are very pink
Pretty flowers do not stink
Beautiful flowers grow from a seed
Beautiful flowers need flower feed
Flower petals are very big
Flower stems are like a twig
Blazing flowers sparkle in the sun
Flowers' pollen tastes like a bun.

Shane Pope (7)

Cosby Primary School, Cosby

Waterfall

Like a crashing avalanche the sky-blue water fell.
The water was a charging bull raging to the ground.
As fast as lightning, the water fell to the vast puddle below,
Running down the cliffs, the water crashed on the rocks.
The water plummeted when it hit the ground,
Jumping off the cliff, the water was as fast as a blink . . .
It was at its destination.

Emily Walker (10)
Cosby Primary School, Cosby

The Sea

The sea
Is as rough as a hungry lion,
Jumps lively,
Is a mad bull,
Is azure like a sparkly jewel,
Is as vast as an extremely large elephant,
Is as long as a snake.

Amy Foules (10)
Cosby Primary School, Cosby

Sword

Sharp, shimmering sword,
Sparkling in the sunlight,
Spiky blade very pointy.

Jewelled handle, very smooth
So shiny,
Like a diamond.

Heather Mills (10)
Cosby Primary School, Cosby

The Harbour

As the large trawler came into the wonderful harbour,
The water rippled gently over the rocky shore.
The water was a graceful fish cutting through the clear blue water.
As quiet as a mouse, the water lay calm and still.
In the distance the water smelt fresh and calm,
Like a beautiful peacock displaying its feathers.

Jonathan McLean (11)
Cosby Primary School, Cosby

Volcanoes

Volcanoes blow, volcanoes are brown
Volcanoes blow in a banging sound
Banging like a rocket
Orange as a sunset
Noisily as a tiger
Bright as the light.

Reece Lockwood (8)
Cosby Primary School, Cosby

Volcano

Volcanoes' lava is hot like the sun.
The lava sizzles all day and all night.
Lava fizzes, ash falls down.
The lava flies high into the sky.
Fire blows up, *bang, boom, bing!*
Fire rushing down.

Charlie Townsend (8)
Cosby Primary School, Cosby

The River

He was from the sea
He went everywhere
There were rocks coming fast
As water lifted them.
Swiftly he flowed
Weaving in and out.

Nicholas Smith (9)
Cosby Primary School, Cosby

Volcanoes

Vicious volcanoes
Exploding everywhere.
Red-hot lava
Bubbling in the air.
Lava running down the volcano!
The ground starts to *shake* when the volcano explodes.

Mae Tyers (7)
Cosby Primary School, Cosby

The River

An astonishing house reflected in the icy water,
A still water drifted down the bank slowly,
The water was like liquid spilling out of the taps,
The rain fell slowly into the icy lake,
The water was a drink that had been spilt everywhere.

Chloe Hawes (11)
Cosby Primary School, Cosby

Flowers

The pretty petal gazes up to the shiny, sparkling sun.
A stripy bee, like a tiger, lands on the flower
and removes all the pollen.
The petal falls off onto the ground.
The sizzling summer ends, the stalk drifts down.

Lois Reeves (8)
Cosby Primary School, Cosby

The Waterfall

The water crashed towards the depths of the sea,
The waterfall escaped with cold liquid,
The constant flowing water abruptly destroyed the banks,
The cool, gushing water hit the rocks like a charging bull,
The water galloped off the gorge.

Callum Shepherd (10)
Cosby Primary School, Cosby

Volcanoes

A volcano is hot like the burning sun.
The flashing flames fly up high.
The ash flies in the sky.
It explodes with a bang like a bomb!

Lewis Smith (7)
Cosby Primary School, Cosby

Desserts

Scrumptious, dreamy
Refreshing, relaxing, shivering
Ice cream, a flake and
A wafer chocolate.

Charlotte Marlow (9)
Cosby Primary School, Cosby

Cats

Fluffy ears, soft ears.
Their beady eyes follow you around.
Their big, black, bulging eyes shine.
Long, licky tongue making a wet, dripping sound.

Sarah Edgson (8)
Cosby Primary School, Cosby

Volcanoes

A vicious volcano bangs like a firework
Flames rush up to the sky, to the sun so high
While the ash crumbles down the volcano
Like rusting stones.

George Ellershaw (7)
Cosby Primary School, Cosby

Beach – Haiku

Bang! Waves crash on rocks,
Rainbows gleaming frantically,
Trees standing proudly.

Charlotte Heggs (9)
Cosby Primary School, Cosby

Snow – Haiku

Relaxed snowy sheet
Sparkling in the scorching sun
Milky and softly.

Anna Blankley (9)
Cosby Primary School, Cosby

A Cat

Milk-slurper
Tail-wagger
Sofa-scratcher
Loud purrer
Lazy sitter
Fish-eater
Rat-killer
Mouse-hater
A cuddly friend.

Myles Dunstan (7)
Dodford First School, Bromsgrove

My Puppy

Fantastic-chewer
Toy-needer
Cat-chaser
Big-pooper
Rubbish-stealer
Slipper-robber
Food-lover

A messy thing.

Emma Smalley (8)
Dodford First School, Bromsgrove

Horse

Water-dripper
Hay-eater
Big-roller
Grass-lover
Fast-galloper
Lovely-cuddler
Deep-sleeper
My best pet.

Beatrice Evans (8)
Dodford First School, Bromsgrove

Dinosaur

Loud-roarer
Animal-hunter
Sharp-clawer
Meat-eater
Bone-cruncher
Jurassic creature
Meteor victims
Extinct.

David (Dougie) Bridge (8)
Dodford First School, Bromsgrove

Guinea Pigs

Furry hair
Carrot crunchers
Cucumber munchers
Water drinkers
Furry friends
Cage runners
Very playful
Animals.

Samantha Cranmore (8)
Dodford First School, Bromsgrove

A Dog

Loud-barker
Tail-wagger
Cat-hater
Food-scoffer
Bin-raider
People-liker
A furry friend.

Lauren Beardsley (8)
Dodford First School, Bromsgrove

Dog

Loud barker
Flea scratcher
Round nose
Lazy sitter
Golly eater

A good friend.

Joe Rolinson (7)
Dodford First School, Bromsgrove

Sea

Sharks swimming
Round us.
Turtles making
Their journey.
Ocean gulls
Screaming.

Isaac Slater (8)
Dodford First School, Bromsgrove

Romans

R ed shields and metal armour ready for battle
O n the hills the opposition stands ready to fight
M en dying
'A ttack!' yells the commander
N umerous men killing others
S un shining . . . people dying.

Jonty David Heslop (9)
Dodford First School, Bromsgrove

Roman

R ed shields and heroic men marching into battle
O n the hills the Celts stand before us ready to fight
M en holding their shields and swords, praying to win the siege
'A rmy, get ready for the attack,' the commander yells
'N ow we fight!' The enemy charges to victory!

Archie Freer (9)
Dodford First School, Bromsgrove

The Elements

Fire

As uncontrollable as an unleashed monster,
As dangerous as a hundred lit fireworks,
As hot as raging anger,
As powerful as a riot,
As big as a city
And as fast as a roaring dragon.

Water

As fast as a speeding whip,
As helpful as medicine,
As uncontrollable as the human spirit,
As cold as a cold-hearted killer, yet
As warm as the gymnastic human's sweat
And as dangerous as the tumbling mountain.

Air

As quiet as the breathless assassin,
As invisible as nothingness,
As much to life as birth,
As powerful as God,
As large as the solar system and beyond
And as important as food.

Earth

As strong as a thousand boulders,
As large as all the mammoths in the world,
As powerful as an army of animals,
As rock-hard as a wrestler,
As smooth as newborn skin
And as still as a stone statue.

The Elements

Jack Clark (9)

Farndon Fields Primary School, Market Harborough

Dogs

Cat chaser
Bone biter
Slobbery licker
Sausage scoffer
Stick chaser
Garden wrecker
Paper getter
Slipper chewer
Mud roller
Crumb eater
Attention seeker
Thief scarer
Tail wagger
Life saver
Sheep herder
Footprint leaver.

What am I?

Gabrielle Jeffrey (10)
Husbands Bosworth Primary School, Lutterworth

Killer Wave — Haiku

The dangerous sea.
One minute calm and peaceful.
The frightening sea.

Aaron Barnett (10)
Husbands Bosworth Primary School, Lutterworth

How Time flies

Time teller,
Tick-tocker,
Wall hanger,
Hand mover,
Hard worker,
Non-stopper,
Sleepy waker,
Minute watcher,
Race timer.

What am I?
A clock!

Emily Kenmore (10)
Husbands Bosworth Primary School, Lutterworth

Little White Horse

A little white horse
came galloping past,
as fast as the wind.
Becoming faster and faster,
gaining more and more
speed until it came
to a stop in the middle
of a clearing.
The moonlight shone
down on that mythical horse
as it became a unicorn.

Isabella Baker (11)
Husbands Bosworth Primary School, Lutterworth

The Jungle

T igers, you will find them here.
H orrible things over here.
E agles fly over you.

J ungle cat will claw at you.
U p over you a cat in a tree.
N othing else will come for me.
G orilla coming over to me.
L aughing hyenas have found me.
E lephants, here they come again,
    everybody is afraid of them.

Tom Ross (11)
Husbands Bosworth Primary School, Lutterworth

Mad About Sports

Football player,
Bad kicker,
Baseball batter,
Splashing swimmer,
Great scorer,
Ice dancer,
Mad runner,
Big jumper.

What am I?
A sports player!

Ruby Blake (10)
Husbands Bosworth Primary School, Lutterworth

My feline friend

Dog hater
Mouse catcher
Tree climber
Silent stalker
Swift killer
Rain hater
Fuss monster
Shrew finder
Loud purrer
Who am I?

Rebecca Bishop (11)
Husbands Bosworth Primary School, Lutterworth

My Rabbit

Hole digger
Carrot cruncher
Speed racer
Mess maker
Furry, funny
Lawn mower
Floppy ears
Kind, fluffy.

What am I?

Leanne Sheasby (11)
Husbands Bosworth Primary School, Lutterworth

The Jungle

T he jungle is bad under the vines.
H orrible things you will hear.
E lephants will stampede over you.

J aguars will jump over you.
U ndergrowth will consume you.
N othing else will come for you.
G orillas take your stuff.
L ions will eat you.
E very day I am glad to be back.

Paul Atkinson (10)

Husbands Bosworth Primary School, Lutterworth

Let's Play Footy

F ootball is awesome.
O bviously the best sport.
O n every day of the week
T here's always a match to watch.
B est day to watch football
A lways a Sunday afternoon.
L eicester are playing.
L et's play footy too.

Kian Gill (9)

Husbands Bosworth Primary School, Lutterworth

Sharks And Cats

Sharks,
Large, vicious,
Scanning, swimming, biting,
Frequently patrolling the landscape,
Exploring, running, pretty,
Small, curious,
Cats.

Carter Gill (11)

Husbands Bosworth Primary School, Lutterworth

Day And Night

Night,
Silent night,
Calm, peaceful, quiet.
Night and day meet.
People rushing round
Bright sun
Day.

Taylor Clarke (9)

Husbands Bosworth Primary School, Lutterworth

Jungle Fever

Jungle,
Damp, lush,
Swinging, chattering, living,
Full of life. No life to be seen,
Whispering, frightening, dying,
Arid, barren,
Desert.

Alexander Garner (10)

Husbands Bosworth Primary School, Lutterworth

Dancing

D ancing, dancing, dancing
A round the living room
N ever stopping, twirling
C an't stop practising
I 've got a show soon
N ot dizzy yet
G etting it right is all that matters.

Candice Hall (11)

Husbands Bosworth Primary School, Lutterworth

A Charm for Good

Ingredients into the saucepan throw,
Lamb is burning when I go.

A dove and a glove
And love from above
Make it and bake it
And have an ice cream dream.

Philippa Ingram (7)
Lea CE Primary School, Ross-on-Wye

Untitled

Mud roller
Muck eater
Ham maker
Pink figure
Animal squasher.

Pig!

Elliot Peeters—Vanstone (8)
Lea CE Primary School, Ross-on-Wye

My Jungle Friend

Vine swinger
Banana eater
Brown hair
Lives in the jungle
Swishy tail.

Monkey!

Megan Berry (8)
Lea CE Primary School, Ross-on-Wye

Untitled

Yellow, fluffy mane
Long tail
Amber eyes
King of the jungle
Brave and proud
Roars loudly.

Nadia Dickinson (8)
Lea CE Primary School, Ross-on-Wye

Untitled

Green and slimy
Glows in the dark
Walks and is see-through
Lives on planet Zonk
And really honks!

Oliver Wiggins—Hay (8)
Lea CE Primary School, Ross-on-Wye

Untitled

Cheeky player
Banana eater
Cage breaker
Vine climber.

Kaitlyn Simpkins (7)
Lea CE Primary School, Ross-on-Wye

Aliens

Slimy blood suckers
They live on the moon
Some have spaceships too
And they live in holes.

Benjamin Carpenter (7)
Lea CE Primary School, Ross-on-Wye

Football Boots

Players' luck
Striking sensation
Always muddy
With studs.

Samuel Bott (8)
Lea CE Primary School, Ross-on-Wye

The Moon Is . . .

A peeled potato shining
in the night.
A golf ball whacked so high.
A football kicked into the
dark goals.
A glowing bauble in a
velvet sea.
A baseball floating
peacefully in the night.
A shining bomb ready
to explode!

Jamie Bowyer (9)
Lord Scudamore Primary School, Hereford

My friends

My friends are really special
And I like them all a lot
They really are the
Nicest friends
That anyone has got.

They help me with my work
They have lovely smiles
I really love my friends
And so should you.

Bethany Proctor (10)
Lord Scudamore Primary School, Hereford

I Wrote Your Name

I wrote your name on a piece of paper
but I threw it away.
I wrote your name on my hand
but I washed it away.
I wrote your name in the sand
but the tide took it away.
I wrote your name on my heart
and forever it will stay.

Brittany Hicks (10)
Lord Scudamore Primary School, Hereford

Rain

Drizzling down the drain, calling out its name,
Rain, rain, rain!
Dripping down the wall, up so high and tall,
Calling out its name,
Rain, rain, rain!
Sliding down the path, soaking up the grass,
Calling out its name,
Rain, rain, rain!

Letitia Rock (9)

Lord Scudamore Primary School, Hereford

The Rainbow

R ainbow in the sky made by bright sun and rain,
A shining gleam of colour dazzling in the sky.
I n the sky a strip of red, blue and green,
N ow it's time to lie on the ground and watch it all day.
B eautiful colours in the sky, shining.
O n weekends it comes out to play,
W indows open wide, it's time to say goodbye.

Charlotte Cooper (10)

Lord Scudamore Primary School, Hereford

Snow

Like crystals drifting from Heaven above,
Single drops, swooping down like a beautiful dove.
A warm white coat covering the town,
The wind blowing the glittery snow with no sound.
Shattering your hair, sparkles here and there,
Tiny pieces of glass, flying high and low.
This is snow!

Megan Trevena (10)
Lord Scudamore Primary School, Hereford

Jaguar

J ust wait a little while
A ll fears will . . .
G o away
U nderneath you
A re jaguars
R un away, run away!

Megan Skivington (9)
Lord Scudamore Primary School, Hereford

Love

L ove is great, you'll never be lonely.
O h how nice, you've bought me a Valentine's present.
V alentine's is great, always getting lovely presents.
E veryone having fun.

Lucie Taylor (9)
Lord Scudamore Primary School, Hereford

The Sun

The sun is like a giant orange,
It is the key to our light,
It brings light to help the flowers grow
And when it goes down it is night.

Josh James (9)
Lord Scudamore Primary School, Hereford

Fagin

Fagin's eyes
Are dead
His skin
Grey and pale
His fingers
Are as dark as ash
Tangled twigs
For hair
He is like
A bundle of
Skin and bones.

Fagin's breath
Forms invisible hands that grasp
Your neck with an embrace
Like singing nettles
His face, hairy and dirty
Like a mouldy kiwi
His laugh
Bubbly
Like lava
His walk, like a creaky door
Talks like a gargling drainpipe.

Madness like an erupting volcano
Exploding bomb
For angriness
Sadness, tears like ocean waves
And happiness like a
Kiss.

Gavin Annis, Achmed, Nikki, Bethany & Destiny (10)
Marriott Primary School, Leicester

Fagin

A collection of
Gritty bones
His eyes are like
Black coal
Dry straw for hair
And a face like burnt toast
Fingernails like
Black
Sticky
Tarmac
His teeth like stale cheese.

Fagin

His breath like
Poisonous
Acid
His grasp like stinging nettles
Dribbles all day like a washing machine
Then laughs like one
His shouts bounce off the wall like gunshots
His nose deeper than the black hole.

Casey Kelly (11)
Marriott Primary School, Leicester

Personification Poem

Another night snoring and
My throat as dry as a desert.
My windows open wide as the
Lamp posts end their shifts.
Bloated dustbins vomit their insides.
Trolleys skate by to go to school,
As phone boxes whistle and whine.
Cars cruise by.

As I walk past,
Benches stretch their lifeless limbs.
Traffic lights wink at them
As they press the button.
Baby dustbins scream at their mothers.
Trolleys skate back home from school.

Fences stand on guard
As lamp posts start their shift.
Litter, begging for a home
As cars cruise by to get home.
Baby dustbins get put to bed.

Richael Ferrie (11)

Marriott Primary School, Leicester

Fagin

A bundle of fragile bones.
His eyes like burning coal.
Hair as dry and dull as stone
And fingers like burnt matchsticks.
His teeth like
Stale
Cheese.

Fagin
His breath attacks like poisonous acid
While his grasp is like stinging nettles.
He dribbles like a broken washing machine
And laughs like a toilet when flushing.
He moves like a clock ticking
Tick-tock, tick-tock.
His shouts bounce off the wall
Like gunshots
Bang, bang, bang!

Chloe Marsden (11)
Marriott Primary School, Leicester

The Tower Block

He stands tall and straight,
As stiff as a statue,
Letting cans tattoo his bleeding walls,
As newspapers shuffle by,
And dustbins hum.

He stomps as he stretches out his limbs,
He waddles and wobbles as he walks,
The tower block clumsily moves around,
As he moans and whines,
And walks with a thud.

He sees trolleys whizzing by, escaping from prison,
Cars waltzing by quietly.
Traffic lights blinking their yellow eyes,
As plastic bags flap their wings around,
And dustbins bloated, as food overflows from their mouths.

Bethany Bell (10)
Marriott Primary School, Leicester

Personification

Cars cruising by,
Houses coughing,
Traffic lights rubbing their orange eyes,
Phone boxes standing guard.

Factories coughing,
Police cars shouting,
Lamp posts moaning,
Baby dustbins wailing.

It smells like a mouldy dustbin vomiting,
It smells of smoke faintly.

It tastes of a liquorice taste,
It tastes of a tarmac taste.

Damien Brooks (10)
Marriott Primary School, Leicester

The Tower Block

How he stands:
He stands stiff and tall,
Watching the city with his glaring windows,
Tattooed walls making him look strong.

What he does:
He wobbles funnily,
He waddles slowly,
He marches to his trolleys.

What he sees:
He sees trolleys skating by,
He sees cars waltzing by,
He sees plastic bags flapping their wings at him.

Nikki Gunn (11)

Marriott Primary School, Leicester

Untitled

I was awoken by the crying baby dustbins.
As I stretched my limbs, the trolleys made their way to school.
Full dustbins vomited all over the streets.

Grumbling to himself, he tried to catch his trolleys.
As I turned around I saw begging litter looking for a home.
Factories coughed.
Cars cruised by from work.
Lamp posts gave me a headache as they snored all day.

Awake all night, I chatted to the bruised and battered wall.
As I tried to sleep the wind waddled me side to side.
As I gently fell asleep the street lights got to work.

Lucy Garner (10)
Marriott Primary School, Leicester

Lightning

A blast of thunder
A shard of lightning
A crack of sound -
I fell to the ground
It struck so hard
It shone so bright
Because lightning is frightening
It crashes and flashes
As it hits metal
So don't go about
It will be lights out!

Matthew Lloyd (10)
Much Wenlock Primary School, Much Wenlock

Natural Disasters

Earthquake appears
Like sharp spears,
Foundations stale,
Death impales,
Towers crumble,
House tumble,
Ground creaks,
People shriek,
Trees fall,
Man and nature brawl.

Volcano explodes
Rids itself of its load,
Lava ejects,
Smoke infects,
Monster rumbles,
People stumble,
Burns out life,
But still more strife,
Death calls,
Man and nature brawl.

Hurricane arrives,
It's come to take lives,
Men don't know,
Until they go,
Winds swirling,
Cars hurling,
Clouds circling,
Water gurgling,
Rips up stalls,
Man and nature brawl.

Benjamin Af Jones (10)
Much Wenlock Primary School, Much Wenlock

A Winter's Day

It was a cold winter's day.
Snowflakes falling from the sky like fairies, sparkling and
                                        twinkling as they fall.
The silent icy wind blows and the leaves fall gently from the trees.

Children playing, with crisp white snow crunching under their feet.
A snowman sitting in the middle of a garden, in a bobble hat
                                        and stripy scarf,
Like an ink blot on a black canvas, as night falls.

As a new dark breaks, children leap from their beds,
Beaming smiles from ear to ear at the sight of the fresh white
                                        layer of snow.
They dash around, pulling on layers of clothes to keep warm,
Racing outside to throw big round snowballs at each other.

The sound of laughter echoes through the icy streets.
The children run and crunch through the freshly fallen leaves,
Enjoying the rustling and crunching as they go.

The sun starts to set and patches begin to appear in the all-white
                                        landscape as the snow begins to melt.
Children sitting around a fire, drying out from their earlier fun.
The lonely snowman slowly melts,
Firstly up to his shiny black buttons, then down to the head,
With his stripy scarf lying on the ground like a snake shedding
                                        his skin.
Eventually, all that is left is a carrot and bobble hat, lying limply in
                                        the middle of the lawn,
Waiting patiently for a new day and a fresh new layer of snow.

Ceyda Ata (9)
Much Wenlock Primary School, Much Wenlock

Devastation

Towers topple like a chair with one leg,
As vigorous quakes strike again,
With evil turning, turning, turning,
Wanting to take more and more,
Why them not us?

Waves charge like a battering ram,
As they collide and shatter defences,
People drowning, drowning, drowning,
Attempting to wipe out mankind,
Why them not us?

Volcanoes detonate like a bomb in Hiroshima,
Pompeii was a fire swamp,
Rising then burning, burning, burning,
Burning them all unfortunately for them
Why them not us?

Land rumbles, rocks and sways like a giant pushing a swing,
With Earth wanting to give way and tumble
Trees falling, falling, falling,
Wrapping up houses as they roll,
Why them not us?

This is horror, unfairness, death at its darkest,
Tragic, painful and breaks many people's hearts,
Just killing, killing, killing,
Countries laid low by these disasters
Why them not us?

James Smith (10)
Much Wenlock Primary School, Much Wenlock

Divorce

Life is different
Life is like war
I'm stuck in the middle
I can't take it anymore.

Mum is shouting, Dad is too
I thought they loved each other
Now all they do is argue.

So worried that I can't sleep
So scared that I can't concentrate
I'm tense so I can't relax
I'm stressed so I can hardly leave my room
Is it all *my* fault?

Dad sleeps on the sofa
Mum sleeps in the bed
No conversation just argument
It's give me a bad head.

I hope they make up soon
I hope they resolve their problems
I wouldn't like new parents
I want to keep my real ones.

Kirsten Jones (10)
Much Wenlock Primary School, Much Wenlock

Polar Bear Crisis

Because of us,
The bears are crying,
Because of us,
The bears are dying,
Because of us,
The fumes we are making,
Because of us,
The ozone layer is breaking,
Because of us,
The ice is crumbling,
Because of us,
The ice is tumbling.

Because of us,
I can't sleep,
Because of us,
Polar bears weep,
Because of us,
The North Pole's a sea,
Now it's down to us,
To make the polar bears be
Free!

Imogen Gullick (10)
Much Wenlock Primary School, Much Wenlock

Divorce

Dad screams
Mum shouts
I am ever so worried

Dad's stressed
Mum's under pressure
It's like a never-ending war

Dad's sick
Mum's upset
They have got so many problems to sort out

Dad says, 'It's your fault!'
Mum says, 'No, it's you!'
Whose side am I on?

Dad packs
Mum's on the phone
They ignore me, don't listen.

Dad says, 'I'm leaving'
Mum says, 'Good!'
'Dad, don't go!'
But he just slams the door.

Amelia West (10)

Much Wenlock Primary School, Much Wenlock

Winter's Weekend!

I am so happy the weekend is here,
It's Saturday morning, I give a big cheer.
It's frosty outside on this cold winter's day,
I must go to the yard, give my pony some hay.
Whilst I have slept in my nice comfy bed,
Jack Frost has been busy, so my mum said.
I go to the yard on this cold frosty morn,
And my pony is happy when I give him his corn.
I put on his tack and I'm ready to go,
I'm feeling so cold from my head to my toe.
I go off, trotting miles down the lane,
Then I look down to see frost on his mane.
A pheasant jumps out of the side,
Oh my goodness, what a scary ride.
The frost on the trees makes me feel very cold,
My pony is scared, he's not very bold.
Back in his stable he gets warm as toast,
He likes to be in there with the things he like most.
Come on Toby, it is all OK,
Get back in the warm and eat your hay.

Katie Doody (9)
Much Wenlock Primary School, Much Wenlock

Bullying

The bullies are laughing,
They do it for fun.
Ow! Stop! It hurts.
Bullying, bullying.
So much hatred,
But still no dread.
They're jealous because I'm good!
Kicking, punching. I wish they'd stop.
Bullying, bullying.

The teacher has found out,
Something's being done.
I've stopped being terrified,
And I like playtime now.
Bullying, bullying.

The bullies got told off,
I've made a friend.
It's all going well.
I hope they don't start it again.
Bullying, bullying.

Eloise Moore (10)
Much Wenlock Primary School, Much Wenlock

Some!

Some live
Some die
Some fight
Some cry
Some shattered
Some not
Some fall
Some small
Some stand tall
Some try to crawl
Some lie dead
Some have scars
Some have guns
Some have mums
Some fight for country
Some fight for honour
Some just fight

But hey
That's war!

Thomas Walters 10)

Much Wenlock Primary School, Much Wenlock

Death Is . . .

Death is so big and so tall,
One way or the other you will fall.
Death will hit you at the door,
When you shriek and give a violent roar.
When you hear that final crow,
You will know you have to go.

Death is such a beast,
It haunts till the end when it chucks you into the pit filled
with fear . . .

Sometimes you will ignore,
The common threat at the door.
Once you've been pierced you won't escape,
While Death decides who next to take.
Death is near
While it impales you with fear . . .

Death hit me yesterday,
My soul was inflamed then claimed by the monster that is
Death!

Samuel Smith (10)

Much Wenlock Primary School, Much Wenlock

Old Lady, Dream Lady

Old lady, dream lady,
Wandering down the street
Pushing a trolley
With no lolly
Carrying bags
Wearing rags
And wandering down the street.

Old lady, dream lady
Wandering down the street
As cars give a *bleep, bleep, bleep.*
Windows open, heads peer
But old lady, dream lady
Just makes a different steer.

Old lady, dream lady
Wandering down the street
She is heading for the bus shelter
Where she'll set up her polystyrene home
I just wonder where she went wrong.

Sam Jukes (10)
Much Wenlock Primary School, Much Wenlock

Winter Wonderland

My steamy breath rises into the bright blue sky,
Ducks slide clumsily on the frozen pond,
Icicles hang from the tall treetops as bright as diamonds,
Excited children squeal loudly all around,
I am ready to plummet down the hill on my shiny new sledge.

Joe Kinton (9)
Much Wenlock Primary School, Much Wenlock

The Effects Of Car Crashes

Terrified and scared,
Burnt up and dead.
Fire consuming
Lives over and over again.
People speeding,
No care for anything,
Cars bashing, crashing, smashing.

Blood everywhere,
People screaming,
People dying,
People praying for their children.

Fire blazing through the windows,
Fire engines rushing to the incident.
Air ambulances taking people
From the crash to A & E.

People who don't take care
Shall face the wrath of being dead!

Alexander Hewer (11)
Much Wenlock Primary School, Much Wenlock

The Wind

The wild windy wind twirls through
The big windows of the big tall tree house wildly.

And while the wind goes through the
Tree house it makes a whistling sound.

It wriggles down my clothes.

Oscar Beavis (9)
Much Wenlock Primary School, Much Wenlock

A Winter's Day

Clear nights bring frost around dawn,
Just as we awaken with a yawn.
Get out of bed with a shiver,
Open the curtains, my body all a quiver.

Windows are covered with feathered patterns of ice,
Icy cold, but look so nice.
I can see my breath, looks like it's airborne,
Quickly get dressed, need to get warm.
Open the door and what do I see?
The most magical sight before me.

Snowflakes, sparkling, six-sided,
Symmetrical shapes softly falling.
Icicles as clear as glass,
As white as a feather, is the grass.
Quietly I stand, my mouth agape,
A white blanket is the landscape.

Stefan Smith (8)
Much Wenlock Primary School, Much Wenlock

The Coldest Day Of The Year

I'm driving to Wales looking at the trees,
They are so frosty, they don't look real.
The fog is as thick as smoky shadows.
We got to Wales and I sprinted to the beach,
The sky was as blue as a whale.
The seaweed was as slimy as a pile of slugs.
It was really the most beautiful day.

Dylan Wheeler (9)
Much Wenlock Primary School, Much Wenlock

On The Street

Nowhere to go
No one to love, I feel sad and I'm in a huff
People pass by then I start to cry
Still I'm cold and wet.

I'm jealous of other 'poshos'
Playing about in the park
But people don't know what goes on outside
With no tea and no bed
Still, I'm cold and wet.

Cold, wet, hungry and lonely
Thin dogs
Fat dogs
Long-haired
Short-haired
But still we're cold and wet!

Chloe Braithwaite (11)
Much Wenlock Primary School, Much Wenlock

A Frosty Winter's Day

In the morning I smelt sizzling sausages,
Inside as warm as toast,
Outside as cold as a fridge,
The ground as slippery as an ice rink,
I see particles of water dripping down the window,
Snow all over the town,
Not a dot of grass to be seen.
Oh I love a frosty, chilly, white, bright day.

Lauren Vickers (10)
Much Wenlock Primary School, Much Wenlock

Icy Land

Icy land, going away,
Polar bears don't want to stay.
All the time, ice is melting,
People don't care, I am worrying.

The wind goes rough, the snow crumbles,
The polar bears run, the ice tumbles.
Cars and fumes, melting the ice,
For the polar bears, it's not nice!

Try to help by walking more,
Do not open the car door.
They'll be happy, so will you,
They will live and you will too!

Icy land, going to stay,
Polar bears, can't go away.

Philippa Neale (10)
Much Wenlock Primary School, Much Wenlock

Cold Winter's Morning

Beautiful trees all covered in snow
The iced pond freezing and gleaming
As it reflects the winter sun
Also the flaky layer of frost
Crunching under my nice warm feet

The ice on the bird bath feels so smooth
And usually smells like mountain air.

Oliver Williams (9)
Much Wenlock Primary School, Much Wenlock

A Winter's Day

The winter passed by
Snow fell from the sky.

Snow fell from the west
And started to rest.

Animals started to rest
Warmly in their nests.

Cobwebs started to freeze
In the cold winter's breeze.

Children played in the snow
Waving their hands to and fro.

So much to see,
So much to do,
Wintertime with me and you.

Hannah Smithurst (9)
Much Wenlock Primary School, Much Wenlock

Frosty Night

I snugly slept
In my bed that night.
Jack Frost nipped outside.
The cold windy breeze
Swept all around the town.
The trees coated with ice
And snow.
One man outside,
His cheeks red as a rose.

Molly Davis (9)
Much Wenlock Primary School, Much Wenlock

Jack Frost's Dance

Look with care on a freezing moonlit night,
The little ice wizard may shimmer into sight.
His cloak swirls and billows as the wizard that is Jack,
Dances this way and that.
He nips at the trees making the leaves glitter
And gleam like diamonds in the moonlight.

As he dances the freeze fairies follow,
Finishing off his valiant work.
Their faces are as white as snow mixed with silvery blue.
Their dresses are ice cobwebs like silk lace,
They are so graceful as they twist and twirl.

Now it is the end of Jack Frost's dance,
As he twirls into the mist,
He gives you a glance, then he winks as he goes.

Niimi Day–Gough (9)
Much Wenlock Primary School, Much Wenlock

Death Of A Soldier

Big bombs flying everywhere,
Rifles shooting at your hair.
The daunting souls hunting you down
As you tremble through the battlefield.
Big bombs flying everywhere,
Rifles shooting at your hair.
The children cry as their family comes back dead.
Why do we need war?
It does not solve anything.

Morgan Stephens (10)
Much Wenlock Primary School, Much Wenlock

The Wind And Rain

The wind, please stop.
You are so heavy,
You are like rain.
The rain roaring roughly
Round rainbows.

Wind, you are hurting
The nature like birds
And you have destroyed
Homes and nests.

The wind, wandering, whistling,
Whirly wildly.
The wind, the wind,
So strong,
So please stop.

Charlie Russell (9)

Much Wenlock Primary School, Much Wenlock

The Effect Of War

The soldier lies still as time stands still,
The gun smiles as it takes a life.
A twisted body lies still on barbed wire.
The nasty bunker sucks life
As dead bodies look pale as can be.
The bullet is horrified of dying,
The salty sand is warm from the footprints of soldiers.
Deep water carries the soldier away
To a faraway place.

Matthew Jon Keith Dyke (11)

Much Wenlock Primary School, Much Wenlock

Cold Winter's Day

On a beautiful frosty winter's day,
The town lies as quiet as a mouse,
While children lie in their warm cosy bed,
Jack Frost nips at the trees.

The fire is crackling before our eyes,
The ruby-red flames are cuddling our hearts.
I hear the milkman treading carefully along the path,
The bottles are clinking in his ice-cold hands.

The sky is as pink as a fresh smelling rose
We feel the cold ice right under our feet.
The sizzling sausages smelling so sweet.
I love such a frosty winter's day.

Katie Hawthorn (10)
Much Wenlock Primary School, Much Wenlock

Why . . . ?

Flowers are wilting, as devastation spreads,
People are grieving, as lives leave.
Confidence full, confidence gone,
This strange monster rumbles on and on.
Mankind wonders - will it ever stop?
Swirling, whirling, killing, round the clock . . .

Death is near . . .

Matthew Hartill (11)
Much Wenlock Primary School, Much Wenlock

A Windy Night

The wind whirled madly around the house,
Nothing was as quiet as a mouse.
The whipping wind howled outside my window,
The wind blew, the house creaked, the bed shook rapidly.

The wind blew the whirling trees outside my window
And I felt cold air on my feet.
The gale outside, horrible and cold,
The wooden door shook, so very old.

How the wind blew, so furiously,
Lots of cold air on my knees.
The sheet was as cold as ice,
Everything so freezing and nice.

Rachel Grace (10)

Much Wenlock Primary School, Much Wenlock

Jack

Jack Frost the little sprite,
Looking around with all his might.
Searching for a leaf or a cobweb
To sprinkle his sparkly, frosty, icy dust.
When day dawns, his work is done.
He has left us icy fun.

Annabel Jane Bald (10)

Much Wenlock Primary School, Much Wenlock

Cold Winter's Day

I'm getting colder every day,
Snowflakes fall softly and slowly.
Snowmen melting day by day.
Some people are lonely, some people are not.
Ponds freezing every day,
People singing, jolly and happy.
People saying, 'Please can you stay?'
Adults are going on walks on a lovely winter's day.
Snowballs being thrown everywhere you look,
Dogs jumping, deer skipping,
Everybody celebrating with a plate of turkey.

Now you can celebrate!

Jake Braithwaite (9)
Much Wenlock Primary School, Much Wenlock

The Wind

The wind blew like a tornado (in the park)
The wind blew quickly (in the night)
The wind howled like a crying wolf (on the beach)
The wind was as gentle as a leaf (in my garden)
The wind was as hard as the rain (in a bird's nest)
The wind was like a feather (in the night).

Phoebe Munro (9)
Much Wenlock Primary School, Much Wenlock

The Wind In A Tree House

The wind whistling like a ghost train, chugging down the line
It sent shivers down my spine
The wind rustling through my hair
Whooshing, twirling without a care
The wind whirling through the trees
With a small breeze.

William West (9)
Much Wenlock Primary School, Much Wenlock

The Windy Rain

O rain why are you such a pain?
Blowing through the windy town.
My children have to put on their gowns.
I think you should win a crown.
O wind, O wind, why do you have to blow?
That's all I want to know.

Rachel Watkins (9)
Much Wenlock Primary School, Much Wenlock

The Brown Horse

He canters across the ground with ease,
No scars to his back or to his knees.
I have a play with him in the field,
No need to have a protective shield.

When I go over a jump on him,
He doesn't knock it with a limb,
'Look at him,' the others cry,
His limit really is the sky.

He has grass as his food,
The horse is never pushy or ever rude.
After he's been ridden, he has a quiet sleep,
I always will have him to keep.

I am never scared of the brown horse,
His mane is so coarse.
Others are scared of him when he runs,
But he will happily share one of my buns.

The brown horse never bites, kicks or bolts,
In a competition he would never get four faults.
He would always get a clear round,
Worth a lot more than just a pound.

The brown horse has taught me all I know,
He will never ever go.
I love the brown horse dearly,
It's just a shame that some others can't see that clearly.

Felicity Spencer (9)
Old Dalby Primary School, Melton Mowbray

Dogs

Dogs, dogs,
They're so, so fun.
Dogs, dogs,
Like you to rub their tum.

Dogs, dogs,
They're so cute.
Dogs, dogs,
Too bad you can't turn them on mute.

Dogs, dogs,
They're so cool.
Dogs, dogs,
They so rule!

Dogs, dogs,
Some fat and small.
Dogs, dogs,
Some thin and tall.

Dogs, dogs,
In competitions they're fast.
Dogs, dogs,
But they can come last.

I love dogs forever
And would abandon one *never!*

Megan Wright (9)
Old Dalby Primary School, Melton Mowbray

My favourite Time Of Year

Christmas is my favourite time,
I love it very much.
Presents given all around
To children and adults.

Children opening presents,
Excitement's all around.
Lots of paper on the floor,
Like snow on the ground.

Christmas trees sparkling,
Bright stars upon the top.
Pretty balls and dazzling lights.
What a pretty sight!

Natalia Platts (9)
Old Dalby Primary School, Melton Mowbray

PlayStation

P erfect fun all day long.
L ove every minute.
A lways looking forward to playing on it.
Y ippee, I played on it all day.
S uddenly I realised my controller was flat.
T rying hard to earn more points.
A ngry when I keep on losing.
T hat's not fair, I cannot play on my PS today.
I 'm always trying to do my best.
O n my PlayStation, three hours, no less.
N o one can beat me!

Jack Addenbrooke (7)
Old Dalby Primary School, Melton Mowbray

Football, Football

Football, football, you play it in the park,
Football, football, never in the dark.

Football, football, I play for Foxes team,
Football, football, we play like a dream.

Football, football, our colours are white, green and black,
Football, football, at training we don't ever slack.

Football, football, my teammates are the best,
Football, football, we are better than the rest.

Football, football, can't you see,
Football, football, is the game for me.

Rory Geraghty (8)
Old Dalby Primary School, Melton Mowbray

Rugby Club

R olling in muddy pitches
U nder sweaty armpits
G irls can play
B oys are always the muddiest
Y oung or old.

C alling out to pass the ball
L aughter and fun
U p and over the post
B alls flying everywhere.

Harry Clayton (8)
Old Dalby Primary School, Melton Mowbray

Untitled

Lazy lounger
Padding paws
Silent creeper
Razor claws
Vicious hunter
Surprise pouncer
Flesh tearer
Magnificent mane
King of pride.

Joel Gamble (8)

Old Dalby Primary School, Melton Mowbray

Ice Cream

I love ice cream
C hocolate or vanilla
E specially with a flake

C ream on the top
R aspberry sauce
E very lick fabulous
A nything will do as long as it is yummy
M y ice creams are always the best.

Millie McKinney (8)

Old Dalby Primary School, Melton Mowbray

My Bedroom

My bedroom is very messy, though sometimes it is very clean.
But when my parents ask me, I don't always seem that keen.
I always try to clean it up
But I just get visits by my tiny little pup.
But then I realise what I do
To make my bedroom as messy as the zoo.
Now I know to keep on track
By always putting my possessions back.

Abbi Addenbrooke (10)
Old Dalby Primary School, Melton Mowbray

Laptops

L aptops are fun to use
A lso you can email on them
P eople are not always safe and sensible on the Internet
T yping, inserting bar charts, painting pictures
O pening some messages can set off a virus
P eople have to be careful with laptops,
                you cannot throw them around.

Tommy Watson (7)
Old Dalby Primary School, Melton Mowbray

Dentists

D entists are helpful.
'E llo, open wide!
N ervous as he checks my teeth.
T eeth clean and sparkly.
I t's exciting.
S tickers if I'm good.
T hat's it, you're done!

Daniella Birchmore (8)
Old Dalby Primary School, Melton Mowbray

Rat

I live in a murky hole.
I'm a thief for food.
I am a tiny animal.
Humans hate me.
People say I am a very dirty animal.
My teeth are so strong that they can cut through metal.

Maxwell Scotland (7)
Old Dalby Primary School, Melton Mowbray

Chinese Dragon

I am very bright and colourful like a rainbow.
I am scary like a monster.
You can see me dancing around the streets like a leaf in the wind.
I jerk my head like a Jack-in-a-box.

Sophie Wisher (7)
Old Dalby Primary School, Melton Mowbray

Snow

S now crunching under your feet as you walk.
N umbing fingers, numbing toes, cold outside as it snows.
O ff the children go on their sledges, laughing.
W hirling snowflakes in the sky, snow is falling from up, up high.

Sarah Parkinson (7)
Old Dalby Primary School, Melton Mowbray

Fish

F ishing for fish at the bottom of the sea,
I love them with chips and ketchup too,
S inging fish songs and wiggling their fins,
H appy all the time when they are swimming free!

Samuel Robinson (8)
Old Dalby Primary School, Melton Mowbray

Animals In The Jungle

There are a lot of animals in the jungle
I can name a few.
The snake was slithering round the tree.
I can hear the humming sound of bees.
Tigers are trying to find their prey.
Creeping and crawling to find food to eat.
I am sure they will stay.
Deer are springing here and there,
Just seen a big brown bear.
Monkeys are climbing up the trees
Swinging from branch to branch,
Eating their bananas as they go.
There they see lots of lizards down below
Walking very slow.
These are a few animals that I thought of.
I'm sure you will find you can do the same.

Gursharan Kaur Atwal (8)
Ravenhurst Primary School, Leicester

Dalek

D estroyers
A ll look the same
L ook out of one creepy eye
E very one the same
K illers.

Jack Philip Roe (7)
Ravenhurst Primary School, Leicester

Animal, Animal

Animal, animal where are you?
I want to come and see you,
You're not my enemy.
Animal, animal where are you ?
You're not my enemy,
You're my melody.
What was I looking for?
You make me feel happy,
When I am feeling sad,
I am so glad I found you,
It has made me feel so glad.
Animal, animal I found you!

Logan Darcy Chapman (8)
Ravenhurst Primary School, Leicester

Butterfly

B lowing around in the gentle breeze, the butterfly shows
its lovely pattern.
U sing its wings to fly around, it collects pollen from all the
beautiful flowers.
T railing pollen behind them, they fly back to their homes.
T rying to avoid the big raindrops, they move side to side.
E njoying the sunshine, the butterflies flutter around.
R oaming free around the world it makes everyone smile.
F litting to and fro, it makes its way around the world.
L ovely patterns spread across its wings.
Y ou can see a rainbow on its wings.

Mae Angela O'Callaghan (7)
Ravenhurst Primary School, Leicester

Happiness

H appiness is the greatest
A ll the faces are smiling
P eople dance when happiness comes to their hearts
P roud to share
I like happiness
N ever alone
E ach heart is to share the joy
S ee how much happiness is in the world
S mile and be happy.

Gemma McLean-Carr (7)
Ravenhurst Primary School, Leicester

The Pig

I am a pig.
I shuffle out truffle.
I'm as pink as a rose.
I have a weird nose.
I have a curly tail.
I look rather pale.
I'm very smelly.
I have a big belly
And that's me.

Clara Mae Hurst (8)
Richard Hill CE Primary School, Thurcaston

The Stars And Me

The planets are round, the moon is bright
But only one thing really caught my eye
The shining glistening star above.
I look up with amazement
There I stood, gazing, gazing up high
I saw a spaceship racing by.
I saw a little light run with glee
I made a wish while it was beside me.
Further and further into the sky
I'm guessing that it's nearly night
As I rest my head on my pillow
I can tell morning is nearly bound.
The moon is round, the planets are bright
But only one thing really caught my eye that night.

Abbi Lowden (9)
St Mary's Bitteswell Primary School, Leicester

School

School is boring
All we do is write.
Write, write, write,
Jabber, jabber into the night.

In the morning
Time to get up.
Mum says, 'Get ready'
But no, no, nope!

Playtime is fun!
Hopscotch or tag.
Now is time to go in
But I just nag, nag, nag.

Lunch is cool
We have huff and puff.
I'm feeling hungry now
Scoff, scoff, scoff!

Home time is the best
Now is the time to get going.
But I remember
I can stop this poem!

Emily Smith (10)
St Mary's Bitteswell Primary School, Leicester

The Eagle

The eagle waits
    For its prey
        To come to it
            And then it pounces
                With the sun
                Behind it
            So its prey can't see it
Then, with its razor-sharp talons
      Opening, it grabs it and
          Goes back to its tree
        To eat it.
           Then it rips its
              Flesh off its bones
            And eats.

Charlie Higgins (10)
St Mary's Bitteswell Primary School, Leicester

The Moon

The moon shines bright
Shining on me
Swimming round the world
In the glittering white light
The sun glows yellow
Glowing on me
Twisting round the sky
Talking to the birds that fly.

Bethan Fletcher (9)
St Mary's Bitteswell Primary School, Leicester

Wintry Landscape

As snow falls
It sparkles and glistens
Shines like the moonlight
Far up in the sky.
Crispy, crackling, crunchy,
Fluffy as candyfloss as it falls.
People run, clatter and fall,
Falling diamonds in the sky
Refreshing and glittery as people glide.
And that's the landscape through my window
So let's just hope it carries on and we will be happy all day long!

Ellie-May Smith (10)
St Mary's Bitteswell Primary School, Leicester

Jelly

Wibbly wobbly jelly
Slides all over the place
If you're not careful
It will get you in the face!
Have it with berries
It's so merry
Have it with ice cream
It's a dream!

Ted Kenton (9)
St Mary's Bitteswell Primary School, Leicester

Chocolate

Chocolate, chocolate,
Delicious chocolate
Melting in your mouth.
Seeing it is tempting
To have a little nibble
It's a lot nicer that Kibble
So try some yourself.

Sam Morris (9)

St Mary's Bitteswell Primary School, Leicester

Wolf

He stalks his prey in the moonlight.
He kills his prey in an instant.
He charges at a thousand miles an hour.
He pounces as high as a skyscraper.
He hides in the tall grass.
He can live in the desert.
He is the *king of the world.*

Daniel Brightmore (11)

St Mary's Bitteswell Primary School, Leicester

Colours

Pink runs up to the sun
Blue eats while he tickles his feet
Red goes to sleep but begins to peep
Orange makes buns but he weighs a ton
Yellow likes to look for a fellow
And purple likes to go round in a circle.

Alice Chambers (10)

St Mary's Bitteswell Primary School, Leicester

Animals

Crazy cats like to have their backs scratched
Daft dogs eat people's socks
Rude rabbits like to eat hay while they sleep in bed all day
Hungry horses like to make a mess
Funny frogs just ribbit all day long
Picky pigs like to take their owner's cigs.

Olivia Sutton (11)

St Mary's Bitteswell Primary School, Leicester

The Washing Machine

When the washing machine is turned on
And the people have all gone
The teeth come out and seek the socks
Chew and munch all in a box.

Nathan Webb (10) & Ryan (11)
St Mary's Bitteswell Primary School, Leicester

Snow

Snow invades the land,
Screaming his way into a battle.
Freezing his enemies on his path,
Applying death,
Then rapidly retreats.

Snow dances gracefully,
Shocking his friends
On his way.
Shining, sparkling
As he finishes his dance.

Snow lies on the ground,
Shivering, screaming,
Trying his best to stay alive.
Trying but he can't,
Melting and flying away.

Shuayb Bajaffer (10)
Shaftesbury Junior School, Leicester

Fog

Fog creeps silently
Throughout the day
Fog not to be spoken to
No civilians do anyway
Cautiously freezing away.

Water on the ground
No longer water
Ice it is
Fog smokes away
Comes again another day.

Fog breathing cold
Not understudied
Driving you mad
Red sky, red nose
Shaking the icy skin-flakes of the human body.

Yasir Mohammed Qureshi (10)
Shaftesbury Junior School, Leicester

Thunder And Lightning

Thunder crashes in the grey clouds
Shining and making a mumbling loud noise
Lightning stomps across the town
Flicking a big light like fire
Spreading around the town
Thunder and lightning work together
To make a big *bang!*

Jasmine Hall (10)
Shaftesbury Junior School, Leicester

Thunderous Rain

Rain drizzles heavily
Spitting water anxiously on the ground,
Invading the earth, humidly as it dances off
Pouring buckets, deluging the city.
The cloud bursts angrily
As it strikes *thunder!*

Rain cries
Dying painfully
As little raindrops are left behind.
The wet grass drying rapidly
And there's nothing left behind

As it swiftly moves up to the clouds,
Cries and runs away
And waterfalls begin to rise.
It goes foggy and it lies down and dies.

Robin Wandia Goodwin (10)
Shaftesbury Junior School, Leicester

Frost

Frost slowly leaps from the clouds,
Tiptoes around the damp ground,
Coating the ground with a transparent plastic sheet,
Camouflages the ground.

Frost grasps ground,
Hoods all land, numbs everything in its way,
Encloses on animals, people, everything,
Frost is a glowing idol,
It is as slippery as a squashed slug.

Frost is a prowling pussycat of ice,
It blankets the ground like a flabby thing.

Marcus Lower (10)
Shaftesbury Junior School, Leicester

Best Friends

B   is for becoming friends
E   is for encouragement
S   is for silent
T   is for technology

F   is for friendship
R   is for respect
I   is for instructions
E   is for education
N   is for nastiness
D   is for demands
S   is for separations.

Neelam Lakhani (11)
Shaftesbury Junior School, Leicester

I Love To Dance

I love to dance
I'd like to go to the top
If I don't dance when I'm bigger
I think I might pop!

I love my dance teacher
She is so cool
I love to dance
It's much better than school.

Milly McCoy (9)
Shaftesbury Junior School, Leicester

Winter Wonderland — Haikus

Christmas starts today
Snowflakes are falling softly
With children playing.

I'm glad school's over
'Cause I can open presents
Then play with them all.

Giving people cards
And building the Christmas tree
Counting tree baubles.

No one can resist
Eating up Christmas dinner
And eating pudding.

Natasha Mann (9)
Thorpe Acre Junior School, Loughborough

Greedy Bees

Greedy bees, greedy bees,
Don't have bobbly knees.
Greedy bees, greedy bees,
Don't like mouldy cheese.
Greedy bees, greedy bees,
Have very bendy knees.
Greedy bees, greedy bees,
Don't have milky cheese.
Greedy bees, greedy bees,
Buzz around in flowery trees
To collect the pollen they need
To be greedy bees, greedy bees.

Rayna—Jade Hutcheon (10)
Thorpe Acre Junior School, Loughborough

Snowflakes Fall Softly — Haikus

Snowflakes fall softly,
Drifting downwards in the sky.
They melt on my tongue.

Snowflakes are freezing,
Drifting gently through the breeze.
They melt super fast.

Snowflakes are all shapes,
Some are small and some are big.
They look like crystals.

Eleanor Godwin (9)
Thorpe Acre Junior School, Loughborough

The War

Switch off the lights,
The siren goes!
Planes start the fight,
Run to the shelter,
As everybody knows.

When all goes quiet and calm,
Wait for the siren,
Then all will be safe from harm.

Libby Ward (9)
Thorpe Acre Junior School, Loughborough

Using My Senses

I like smelling melted chocolate and eating it with marshmallows.
I like watching popcorn popping and then watching a DVD.
I like walking through a field of roses and feeling them tickle
across my leg.
I like touching a really fluffy dog and giving it a bath.
I like seeing baby cubs at the zoo and stroking their soft fur.
I like listening to the wind on my window when I'm tucked up in
my blanket.

Reem Oulad (9)
Thorpe Acre Junior School, Loughborough

Using My Senses

I like smelling freshly cut grass and then walking through it.
I like watching cheese melt on toast and pretending it's lava.
I like walking through long grass as it sways in the wind.
I like touching bark on a tree and watching it sway.
I like seeing light reflecting on a car as it shines.
I like listening to wind blowing and rustling.

Alex Halford (8)
Thorpe Acre Junior School, Loughborough

The Beautiful Butterfly

Butterflies are so colourful
Oh how wonderful
Colours are glittering
Patterned wings are fluttering
Oh how beautiful.

Jessica Mistry (8)
Thorpe Acre Junior School, Loughborough

My Life As A Piece Of Paper

A girl picked me up
Put me on a desk.
I felt the light hit me
As an office man walked in.
He picked me up
I was filled with excitement,
I knew I was going to get used
But for what?

My nightmare began
When he put me in the printer,
Where it pinched my back
And dabbed ink on.
Finally I was out
But it wasn't over yet.
He stuffed me in an envelope
Suffocating me as much as he could.
I knew that soon when I was opened
I would go to the place all papers fear . . .
The *shredder!*

At last I was opened,
I must have been a bill
Because of their complaints.
My heart was thudding
So fast I couldn't stop it.
I knew she was going to do it
She did!

I am now over the shredder
Waiting to die as she pushes me in.
I'm half way in . . .
It's strange seeing my bottom cut into eight.
Every bit of my body is now cut.
Help! (Dead!)

Karya Sipahi (10)
Trinity Primary School, Hereford

The World Around Us

When I look around me
I see beauty everywhere.
I see a wonderful place
Which needs our love and care.

When we plant a seed,
The rain will always fall.
The sun will always shine
And a tree will grow tall.

The tree gives us oxygen
So that we can breathe.
The flowers contain nectar
For the buzzing, buzzing bees.

We would die without those trees
Just take a minute to think.
Without the things we take for granted
We would be extinct.

Let's go for it everyone,
We can do this together.
By doing simple little things
We can stop the changing weather.

Turn off that light
When you leave the room.
If we do this simple task,
The world will thank us soon.

Fruit and veg in the compost,
Recycle your paper and plastic.
Glass, clothes, shoes and cans,
Bottles would be fantastic.

The green grass, the sky,
The sea so deep and blue.
One day you could say
It's still here because of you.

Phoebe Mills (10)

Trinity Primary School, Hereford

A Snowflake's Life

As I tumble to my doom,
Out of that wonderful warm cloud,
I fall and fall and fall,
Faster and faster,
I can't stop and I start to panic.

Hey wait . . .
Suddenly I see the grass,
That soft, lush grass.
It looks so welcoming,
I long to touch it.

The grass is softer than it looks,
It must be Heaven.
Yeah, I just know it.

After minutes of dreaming
Reality hits me.
I'm put in a glove along with thousands more,
It all goes dark . . .
I'm scared!

I see sunlight again,
There's hope for me.
Wait, what's happening?
To my horror I'm thrown!

I and the other flakes smash against a body,
Oh no, have I hurt them?
Surprisingly they start to laugh,
I think I've made someone happy.
My life as a snowflake has been fulfilled.

But . . . no . . . the sun has come out!
I start to cry as I look at myself and realise I'm nothing more
than slush!

Olivia Williams (11)
Trinity Primary School, Hereford

My Life As A Pencil Case

The zip was drawn
And I felt fresh air
I was pulled out
And set down on the desk
I filled with excitement
As I was about to be opened
But I knew
It wouldn't last.

My nightmare began
As I was turned upside down
And my contents
Were dropped out
My heart deflated
Like a car tyre
I knew I would be going
To the place
Pencil cases dread . . .
The bottom of the school bag!

As if that wasn't enough
I was filled up again
But even more was added.

I felt like I was going to burst
My stitches started to stretch
And as sure as the sky is blue
I was lifted up
And crammed into
The bottom of the school bag!

Ruairidh Wood (11)
Trinity Primary School, Hereford

My Life As A Laptop

The cabinet opened,
Light burst in.
I was fully charged,
This was my chance.
My charger got pulled out
I felt the massive hands pick me up.
I lay on the table ready
Then I got turned on
But I knew I'd be put back in the dreaded cabinet.

But then, horrors of all horrors happened.
The stupid human
Dug its fingers
Underneath my key.
My 'K' got picked off!
At this moment
I felt my heart drop,
I might have to be replaced!

Then even more torture,
The careless child
Brought its drink over
Without a care
It spilt on me!
My life as a Dell computer was over.

James Rouse (10)
Trinity Primary School, Hereford

My Life As A Pencil Case

Boing, boing, boing!
I'm inside this dark schoolbag
I filled with joy
We're nearly at school
And I'm about to be opened.
A hand plunges in
And takes out a pen.

My heart sinks
As she fills me with more pens
And my body expands.
I feel like I'm going to *pop!*
Suddenly I feel a hole inside me
And my contents charge out.
I know I'm going to the place
All pencil cases dread . . .
The bin!

I feel a hand plunge inside me
And empty the remaining contents.
I feel empty and alone.
I get a cold shiver down my spine
The hand grabs me
And down I go into the bin!

Oliver Blunn (10)
Trinity Primary School, Hereford

The Candle

The everlasting flame is fierce at thee
The flickers are fierce as it rages at me
The scolding hot flame is madder than ever
The flickering flame has nothing to fear.

It braces itself like a tiger ready to pounce
The flame is ready and doesn't mess around
It warms the room with its deadly smoke
The flame is near and ready to attack.

Be careful young one, it has a deadly attack
With one flicker you're in a deadly spot
The flame flickers at thee
And scars thee for life.

I kill the flame with a blow of oxygen
The flame flickers one last time
The flame gets smaller, smaller, smaller
The flame gets smaller by the second.

It tries to stay strong but it is too weak
It suffers pain and disappears
The flame is no longer
And doesn't come back.

Amy Harris (9)
Trinity Primary School, Hereford

A Snowflake's Life

I rest in a cloud sleeping,
Waiting here to be frozen.
Getting colder and colder in the minus temperature,
I dream of falling from the sky.

A crack appears in my bed,
Drifting, floating, falling down through the air.
I am as cold as ice
And then I reach the blanket of snow.

I lie dormant waiting to be played with,
The grass pokes and prods my skin
As more snow crystals fall from the sky.
Then a stampede leaves their marks.

I hate being trampled on
And being crumpled into snowballs.
It makes me laugh when snowmen have a carrot stuck in their face
But it is not funny when that snowman is me.

My play days are over as I grow old,
Children don't want to play no more.
My body freezes over,
Now I am just slippery slush.

Evie Skyrme (10)
Trinity Primary School, Hereford

Clock

The lights flicker
On, the beautiful teacher
Walks in filling my
Heart with joy! I
Hear laughter in
The background, all of
The children rushing
In. I wish I could be
A watch, oh the things
I could do and see,
It would be amazing
But no, all I see is
A classroom day in
Day out. No one ever
Looks no one cares
For me, no one!
I dread that day
When my *tick-tock*
Of a heartbeat
Stops and my life
Ends horribly!

Megan Farr (11)
Trinity Primary School, Hereford

My Life As A Reading Book

Cold hands grabbed me, I was pulled out of my slot.
Instantly I was being carried over to the table.
As soon as I knew it, my pages were being opened and
a face peered in.
I could see the light so soon
My pages were being flicked too quickly for a normal book
She wasn't reading the words but I felt happy I was being used.

This girl wasn't nice, she tore my pages out
That was the best part of the book, why did she do this?
Suddenly she carried me over to the teacher.
The teacher said, 'This isn't good, it will have to be sold.'
Sold, so soon! My nightmare had started. What would happen
to me now?
I didn't want to be sold, where would I go?

The class filed out, the teacher snatched me up.
She took me to her car and popped me in a box.
On the weekend she put me up for sale in a car boot sale.
Suddenly a lady bought me and took me to her house.
Instead of reading the rest of my pages she put me on the fire!
My short life had come to an end.

Tillie Kendall (10)
Trinity Primary School, Hereford

The Frost Dragon

The frost dragon is so cold,
The frost dragon is so bold.
See him flying in the sky,
See him flying in your eye.

See him flying to the west,
Isn't he just the best?
See him soaring in the sky,
See him soaring in your eye.

If you see him in his cave
You must be so very brave.
If you see him flying low,
He will be the first to know.

See him eating in his cave,
Isn't he just so very brave?
See him gliding in the sky,
See him gliding in your eye.

See him flying in the night,
See him flying in the light.

William Blackman (9)

Trinity Primary School, Hereford

There's A Fire In The Forest

There's a fire in the forest
The creatures are fleeing
The flames close behind
With the wind driving onward
From underbrush up to
The high moving treetops
The fire's surging forward
There's a fire in the forest
The whole woods are burning
The creatures are seeking
The safety of streams
Beyond the hot burning
The creatures are fleeing
They are labouring, straining
To reach the cool river
They know it's just beyond them
To escape the fierce burning
To reach the cool stream
For which they are yearning.

Calum Loveridge (10)
Trinity Primary School, Hereford

My Life As A CD Player

The light flashed as I rubbed
My eyes ready to be used
I knew for one moment
That Miss Ross would finally turn me on
But I hoped it was calm music
And I was filled with excitement.

My nightmare began
When a dinner lady unplugged me
And replaced me, replaced me with a Hoover!
I felt upset with no power
Lonely and scared
Would Miss Ross notice or would I end up
In the dark cupboard?

The moment arrived
She picked me up and slowly
Walked towards the dark, dusty cupboard
Is this the end?

Hayden Boulton (11)
Trinity Primary School, Hereford

Ladybird

Lovely ladybird sat on her own
As red as a ribbon with black spots also
She cried out, 'Is somebody there?'
I went up and said, 'Hello there.'
Poor little ladybird who once was alone
But not anymore because I'm taking you home.

Kylie Hopkins (9)
Trinity Primary School, Hereford

My Life As A Shoe

The cupboard door opened and the light shone in.
I felt the air hit me as I was dragged out of my sleeping place.
I couldn't wait to be used but who by?
Excitement poured in through me as
I knew I was going to be cleaned by the smooth, shiny, shoe polish.

I finally was placed on the kitchen floor and the children piled in.
She crunched down on the backs of my heels and made creases
and folds.
The foot sank and I cried in pain as she pushed in her fat foot
And I knew I wouldn't last long, I would be taken to the awful place
that all shoes fear . . . the bin!

If that wasn't enough, she stamped on me sending horrible thoughts
all around my body
And hurting me so much I knew something had happened to me.
After that horrible moment I looked at myself in shock.
My body was totally ruined but that wasn't the end,
She walked outside heading to my worst nightmare . . . dog poo!

Beatrice Rose (10)
Trinity Primary School, Hereford

Garden

Ants crawling everywhere, scatter, scatter, scatter.
Plants growing everywhere, grow, grow, grow.
People stamping on the grass, stamp, stamp, stamp.
Worms sliding, sliding everywhere, slide, slide, slide.
Frogs hopping everywhere, hop, hop, hop.
Birds singing everywhere, sing, sing, sing.

Lydia Willis (7)
Trinity Primary School, Hereford

Homework Again

Tom forgot his homework
It's over in Timbuktu
Katie isn't here
She moved to Peru.

Rolo, Kat and Ellen
Drive teach around the benders
Sophie was too busy
She was watching EastEnders.

Rosie didn't get it
It made her brain churn
Whilst Jay wanted his maths
To crackle and burn.

A small voice whimpered
'I've done mine Miss!'
Now teach thinks she's a saint
Someone call an ambulance, the teacher's gonna faint!

Jasmine Winter (11)
Trinity Primary School, Hereford

Wonderful Light

The sun said goodbye to the moon at night,
Then yawned as she woke up in the morning light.
She balanced above the world,
As she moved, she turned and curled.
Her beam of light she gives to us,
Like turning on a torch with no fuss.
If you look above your head,
Through the clouds you are led,
To the beaming light that your eyes can see,
For only you and me.
But if you look too hard she can hurt and kick,
Makes you cry and makes you sick,
But when the clock moves on
We say goodnight,
To the person who gave us . . .
Wonderful light.

Ellie Reid (11)

Trinity Primary School, Hereford

The Rockets

The rockets are lit
Up, up they go
With silver ash falling.
Then red, yellow and sometimes blue
Bursts into a flower
That's grown to a hundred metes tall.
Then slowly they fall
To the ground in silver petals.

Jake Mills (10)

Trinity Primary School, Hereford

My Life As A Pencil Case

I saw the lights go on in the classroom
And I knew children were going to open my zip.
When the children opened my zip, the air barged in.
I felt a pencil being slowly dragged out of me,
What was going to happen to my new friend?

My nightmare began as the elbow knocked me off the table.
Lucky me, he caught me and put me back on the table.
Phew, that was a relief!

For some reason someone was opening and closing my zip.
Oh no, my second fear!
What was going to happen to me?
What was going to happen to me?
Then he stopped, a bell rang.
Then he grabbed me and chucked me in the air.
The children left, ready for tomorrow.

Ryan Taylor (10)
Trinity Primary School, Hereford

Hiding

You can't see me, I'm hiding, here I am,
I'm hiding again! Bet you can't find me this time.
Under a bush in the garden is a very good place to hide,
So is a big umbrella or down at the end of the bed.
Sometimes Dad hides behind a newspaper
And Mum hides behind a book on the sofa.
My favourite place to hide is behind the kitchen door
Then I jump out, 'Boo!'

Rachel Freeman (9)
Trinity Primary School, Hereford

My Life As A CD Player

The dusty cardboard box doors opened up
And I came into the light of the outside territory
I got dragged out by my smooth handle
So glad to be back in the fresh air again
But I knew this would come to an end soon!

My nightmare began, I got slammed onto the table
Her fingers fumbled around with my stiff buttons
She opened my head with one hard punch of the open button
She put a Katie Melua CD in, *aah,* it was soft music!

My head was clasped back together
I could feel the rough CD turning round
I started to feel dizzy and tired
I felt the green button turn to red
My nightmare had come true; I was broken!

Amelia Daw (11)
Trinity Primary School, Hereford

My House

Outside my house there is a woodlouse,
Under my house there is a mouse.
In my house there is me standing by my daddy.
On top of my house there is a bird
Which is silent, it does not like to be heard.
In the lounge there is my brother
Watching TV with my mother.
There is a connection with us all apart from the woodlouse
Which is now outside my door.

Elizabeth Tate (9)
Trinity Primary School, Hereford

My Life As A Folder

A hand grabbed me, I was ready to be opened.
They moved me out of my nice warm home
I was free from agony and pain, ready to be stretched.
They passed me around the class but where were they taking me?
The nightmare began when a boy threw me on the floor
                                              and stood on me,
But it just got worse!
He scribbled and put messy paper in me, I was really, really angry,
I hoped I wouldn't be in the rubbish bin!

Well, as sure as day is day he kicked me near the bin.
I was really, really scared.
At that very moment my friends and family were thrown in the bin!
Then it happened; he threw me into the bin!
My short life was already over.

Melissa Fitzmaurice (10)
Trinity Primary School, Hereford

Anne Frank

Cold as ice
Staring into space
Lonely, no one to play with.
Tired, no privacy!
Thirsty, hungry,
Sad.
Seeing the same faces, *boring!*
Dreaming of freedom hopefully,
Cramped, dying to get out!

Courtney Bishop (11)
Trinity Primary School, Hereford

My Life As A Literacy Book

A hand fumbled in the box and I was lifted out.
I felt the breeze rustle my pages as she slid me onto the table.
My pages were flicked through as she found the right page.
Exhilaration brushed my spine; it was my time to shine.

Horror!
She grabbed the coloured crayon, she recklessly scribbled
on every single page.
When she'd finished with the pages she had a go at the cover!
I felt abused, ambushed although I had no better use than
to be crayoned on.

As if I hadn't been punished enough
She tore me in half and threw me into my final resting place . . .
the bin!

Aislinn Olivia Lock (10)
Trinity Primary School, Hereford

In My Fridge

A bottle of squash
Some lettuce to wash
Peanut butter and jam
One egg and some ham
Chicken and cheese
A jar of honey from bees
Chocolate cake and cream
It must be a dream
I must get food out of my head
Oh no, it's time for bed!

Olivia Russell (7)
Trinity Primary School, Hereford

Dolphins

The delightful dolphin
Swims silently in the moonlight sky
Swirling, curving, tossing like a flying Frisbee
As the moon shines
At its brightest.

Shining elegantly as he swims
Chasing tuna for his hungry belly
Splashing all of his friends
Swimming calmly back to his family.

Listening to the waves crashing
Dreaming peacefully
As the sun goes.

Lily Corner (11)
Trinity Primary School, Hereford

My Cat

I look out the window
Mittens is crouched low
My cat loves to play and leap in the hay
Whenever I call she comes my way
She climbs on a wall
And she stands so tall
When she looks down at me I feel small
When she curls up she looks like a ball

She looks up at the sky
As a bird makes a cry
She's off like a shot
Will the bird care a lot?

Emily Richardson (9)
Trinity Primary School, Hereford

Fallen Giant

F allen tree
A nyone want to come and play?
L ying helplessly on its side
L onging for someone to discover its branches
E ager for squirrels to scamper round its trunk
N o one to feel its scaly bark and gooey sap

G roups of children come running happily to nature's playground
I ce in winter resting on the ragged roots
A nimals shelter in the hollows of the magnificent fallen giant
N ight hawks swoop round the twisty, twirly branches
T he tree is content.

Martha Hitchin (9)
Trinity Primary School, Hereford

My Pet

Tail wagger
Trouser biter
Food eater
Ball catcher
Great swimmer
Fast runner
Shoe stealer
Small puppy
Big monkey
That's my friend.

Jack Dean (7)
Webheath First School, Redditch

Animals

Horses are neighing
Dogs are barking
Cats are eating fish
Rabbits are hopping and playing
Cheetahs are cheating and running
Lions are eating meat
Tigers are panting and running
Bears are happy eating sweet honey
Panthers are purring.

Luisa Churchman (7)
Webheath First School, Redditch

Feelings

Mouth smiling
Eyes crying
Unhappy child
Happy smile
Sad face
Silly laugh
Shy eyes
Unkind, nasty
That's how we feel!

Rebecca Newby (7)
Webheath First School, Redditch

The Club Whacker

Club whacker
Hole scorer
Flag waving
Good aiming
Ball losing
Driving hard
Putting light
Getting ready
A good sport.

William Skelton (8)
Webheath First School, Redditch

What My Dog Does

My dog goes *woof* all around me,
She steals the socks and chews them up,
She eats the dog food, *gobble, gobble, gobble.*
She licks my face, lick, lick, lick.
I take her for a walk every day,
I give her a bath too.
Then three years later puppies come by,
They are just like her.
That's my dog.

Lauren Rowley (8)
Webheath First School, Redditch

A Hungry Tiger

A fierce tiger ferociously roaring
Speeding tiger to its prey
He runs like a five hundred metre sprint
I bet he will win the prize
The hungry tiger ready to roar
His mouth is wide open
But watch out, the tiger is ready to bite
Snap! The prize is his.

Isaac Jaya (8)
Webheath First School, Redditch

Mythical

M inotaur
Y eti
T yrannosaurus Rex
H enchman
I carus
C reature
A mphibian
L ion Man.

George Clements (7)
Webheath First School, Redditch

The Rumble

The jungle rumbles
Up and down
Side to side
All around
It's noise and sound
The monkeys dance
Like kangaroos.

Ryan Kelly (7)
Webheath First School, Redditch

Hamsters

H amster are cute
A mazing climbers
M ini tongues
S liding down the slide
T asting sunflower seeds
E ating peanuts for his dinner
R unning around the cage.

Faye Curnock (8)
Webheath First School, Redditch

Animals

A is for an alligator
N is for a newt
I is for insect
M is for mammoth
A is for an ant
L is for lions
S is for spiders.

Rebecca Wilkins (8)
Webheath First School, Redditch

The Sea

T he black, dull sea
H overing through the sea
E nd of the sea

S wishing through the weeds
E ating through the sea
A tlantic all blue and fishy.

Zoe Finney (7)
Webheath First School, Redditch

Feelings

Feelings, feelings,
If only I had feelings.
If only I could be funny,
Silly, cheeky, naughty, stupid too.
I wish I had feelings, I do.
Then I could be like you.

Faith Mowat (7)
Webheath First School, Redditch

My Rabbit

R abbits chew things
A nd do lots of poos
B eing naughty, going through holes
B eing good, mostly staying at home
I n a long house
T hat's where rabbits live.

Megan Hawkes (7)
Webheath First School, Redditch

Sharks

S ome people say run like the wind, but they swim like the wind
H elp me get away, out of the shark's way
A tooth fell in the water
'R un,' I shouted
K eep being a shark fan
S harks are dangerous.

Jasmine Randall (8)
Webheath First School, Redditch

Tree Poem

I started off as a tiny seed
But now I am very large indeed.
Just bigger than a grain of sand
When I was buried in this land.
With water, sunlight helping too
I have grown as big as you!

Alexander Stronach (7)

Webheath First School, Redditch

What Animals Do

Rabbits are hopping
Tigers are running
So many things they do.
Birds soaring in the sky
Rats squealing in the drainpipe
There are so many things they do.

Hollie Greaves (7)

Webheath First School, Redditch

Lazy Cat

My cat is very lazy, this is what she does:
She jumps through the cat flap just to have fun.
Then she curls up by the fire and starts to play dead.
Then she jumps on the shed and waits to be fed.
I give her crunchy biscuits and hope she will go to bed.

Ellie Moss (8)
Webheath First School, Redditch

Space

Roaring rockets race through space
Planet to planet they go
UFOs go raving by shooting lasers to slow each other down
The moon is made of green cheese
Everyone loves cheese, especially cheddar.

Thomas Stanton (8)
Webheath First School, Redditch

Football

Running, scoring, getting a red card,
Waiting on the bench for a chance.
Practising for the match, waiting for a catch.
'Catch that ball!' is screamed.
The referee blows, it's the end of the match.

Daniel Morris (7)
Webheath First School, Redditch

The Silly Cat

The cat is eating curry
And is in a big hurry
He runs round the room
Holding his huge tummy.

Nathan Daniel Jenkins (8)
Webheath First School, Redditch

The Fun Jungle

In the mighty jungle there is lots to do
Jumping, hopping, skipping
Swinging from branch to branch in the mighty jungle.

Tom Watson (8)
Webheath First School, Redditch

Bumblebee

Bumblebees *buzzing, buzz, buzz, buzz!*
They're pretty in yellow and black
Buzz, buzz, buzz!
Always long, sucking up nectar from
Red, yellow, pink, white, violet, blue and purple flowers
Going *buzz, buzz* in every direction
To make the tastiest honey there can be.

Noreen Mulla (8)
Wyvern Primary School, Leicester

My Special Friend

Friendship is like a flower
Growing in its glory
Each and every seed
Telling its own story.

As each flower develops
And then continues to grow
More of its strength and cleverness
Continues to show.

And like a garden
It shows much more fair
When carefully looked after
By those who care.

Once in a while
You come beside a friend
Who is as bright as a flower
With a good heart to lend.

So I picked this flower
And pulled it separately
And soon all its pieces
Grew into me.

But then what I realised
Is that this flower that grew
Was not leaves and petals
But pieces of you.

Your help and kindness
Your strength and goods
Have helped me grow
Into my own little flower.

And now with our friendship
I'll never let it go
And spread the word so more
Flowers know.

Bhavni Tailor (10)
Wyvern Primary School, Leicester

Snapeegator

(Inspired by 'Jabberwocky' by Lewis Carroll)

'Twas brillig colding and thous slithy toes
Bonognoves, gnye and grimble away through
Tho tulgly woods
And the mame maths outrages.

Beware the snapeegator my souls!
Thou jaws that snap to catch
Thou claws that clasp to also catch
Beware thou clam fram bear and shun down fest.

Souls awaged therecious sword
Thou time through they foe he craught
She nested by the rumtum tream
In creepless thought.
Trip trop trop mod outgrabe thous snapeegator!

In ugliest thought he stood
Thum thump the eyes of dramsticks.
Came fumious with lighting
And blurbed with stisky breath.

Fee two, five one, and through and through
The noble blade went biccar back
He left it nest for the best
Then with its head went thuming back.

And, has thou slin the snapeegator?
Rise thou arms my grablouls boy!
Hallay! Hallay! He monched in joyness!

Simarpreet Badyal (10)
Wyvern Primary School, Leicester

Saphira The Cave Dragon

As she dug claws into the cave ground
She close by heard the howl of an Irish bloodhound
The cave echoed, 'Is this your life - complete violence?'
Although he was brave and fierce
He felt like his heart had been pierced!
He was the last of his kind
And the thought of dying brought fear into his mind
The archer arrived, mind fixed on his prey
Sanding tall, not afraid
The next second the arrow flew through the air
And Saphira felt like she was in a pit of despair!
From then on she knew it was her fate to die
So as the wolves tore and ate her flesh, she didn't cry
The cave didn't want to lose its only resident
The arrow's blood-red tears trickled down her shivering scales
And so her heart was pierced by the archer's fine arrow
And so it was Sahpira, the greatest dragon of them all died.

Manveer Singh (10)
Wyvern Primary School, Leicester

Hop, Hop, Hop Just Like A Rabbit

To keep a rabbit is a good habit
A rabbit is truly curious
His eyes are soft but his whiskers wriggle and his ears jiggle
And his tail is a bump on his rump
A rabbit is cheerful but not especially careful about multiplying
The answer he gets to the simple sum
So if you get the change to have a rabbit, grab it!

Purvi Chamunda (10)
Wyvern Primary School, Leicester

Slifer The Sky Dragon

(Inspired by 'Jabberwocky' by Lewis Carroll)

As the smight fighs slumpered along the fields of the countryside, they murmured,
'He will come again and taken another of us!'

'Beware the mouth that burns, the tail that stings my farless boy.'
'Yes father.'

There the boy stood in doupth through by the frim tree awaiting the dragon
There it came whifflign through the woods with eyes of anger.
With a wiff waf the boy seized the dragon's head gripping back to his father
'Come here my blinding boy trip, trip, tooray!' For the father was amazed!

The fighs did not worry more about the fremetress dragon for it was no longer alive.

Aaron Dhillon (10)
Wyvern Primary School, Leicester

Winter

Winter, winter,
The great winter
Snowing, cold
Winter, winter
If you see winter
Don't forget to scream
I love winter.

Rehmat Sotta (7)
Wyvern Primary School, Leicester

The Stars

Swirling and whirling,
Shining with light,
Jumping around in the dark, dark night,
Dancing around in sight.
Now you can see
That they are sparking with glee.
Their silver hands and feet that come to town,
Right to the ground.
To keep an eye,
They say goodbye.
Before they went
They saw a tent.
He saw the star book
And had a look,
That he took.

Ravina Shah (11)
Wyvern Primary School, Leicester

Hallowe'en Poem

You can rap about a witch on her broom
Zooming, zooming to the moon.
You can rap about the kids in the street
Collecting some yummy sweets.
You can rap about the kids in the streets
Picking up their trick or treat.
You can rap about a witch dancing in a ditch.
You can rap about a witch sleeping in a tree.
Boom! It's only me!

Rajveer Singh (7)
Wyvern Primary School, Leicester

The Maze By The River

There's a maze by the river,
The spooky, spooky river.
There's a vicious witch that rules,
She rules the bats and the wicked rats
And the spookiest ghost of all.
She rules the cat that sat on a mat
And the scariest goblins of all.
She rules the child that hit the witch and
The car that lost its parts like the
Spooky gears and the steering wheel
And the scariest wheels of all.
But now my poem is at an end
So do not ask for me my friend
So be quiet so I can run away
From that scary, spooky, ugly, smelly, vicious witch.

Arrjun Ramkumar (7)
Wyvern Primary School, Leicester

Summer

Summer is coming, summer is coming,
Let's celebrate and play.
You get to go out in no snow or rain,
As we play the sun shines down on us.

Jump out of bed, don't be lazy,
Let's go and play it's summer today
Summer is a time of no rain, no snow,
Only the big sun shining at you.

Shayna Patel (9)
Wyvern Primary School, Leicester

My Life

I have a life
It's worth more than a knife.
My life, my nose, my look,
I love reading a book.
I beg, plead and try
I even know how to fly.
I eat soup, chocolate, that's all
Hobbies, obviously playing with a ball.
Exercise for me is dance
My sister likes to prance.
My brother always trades
Mostly at parades.
I always make calls, *ring, ring*
What's your life about?

Karishma Supeda (9)
Wyvern Primary School, Leicester

A Cooking Poem

Cooking's my thing in the kitchen or in the court
Laugh if you want, because I'm a good sport.
Don't mess with me when I've got the ball
Because you'll be heading for making a fall.
Fiery so that no one can stand my heat
In the game all the others look beat.

Gurneet Bhars (9)
Wyvern Primary School, Leicester

Snowflake Poem

When me and my friend see a snowflake fall,
My friend says, 'That one is very small.'

Snowflakes fall in the country and city
But no matter where you are
They are always very pretty.

Snowflakes, glittery from the sky.
Snowflakes, snowflakes up so high.
Snowflakes, snowflakes, soft and white.
Snowflakes, snowflakes, a beautiful sight.

Little snowflakes we saw today,
Next time we will see them
I think it will be Monday.

Nidhi Chauhan (7)
Wyvern Primary School, Leicester

The Summertime

The afternoon had got hot
Eyes blurred and closed
And sweating arms
And hair blown.

I sat in the park
After the six hours of school
June walked away
And July came again.

The day came colder
And still sitting
July went to bed
And started knitting.

Hajra Sotta (10)
Wyvern Primary School, Leicester

Funny Animals Around The World

I saw a monkey sitting on Mars.
I saw a dog jumping on cars.
I saw a cat chewing a bone.
I saw a donkey at home
And I saw a horse reading his big book of jokes.

I saw a pig cooking a dish.
I saw a squirrel munching a nut.
I saw an ape hugging a huge shape.
I saw a fish eating the pig's dish
And I saw a slug in my mug.

Suman Mal (9)
Wyvern Primary School, Leicester

I'm Practically Perfect In Every Way

I'm practically perfect in every respect
I haven't a flaw you could ever detect.
As soon as you know me I'm sure you'll agree
There's no one around who's as perfect as me.

I'm beautiful and rich with a generous heart
I'm funny and charming and totally smart.
At school in my classes I only get As
I'm also athletic in so many ways.

My clothes are expensive, my hair is just right
My teeth are all straight, they're shiny and white.
I'm practically perfect, I'm sure you could tell
And oh, did I mention? I'm humble as well.

Nikkita Gokani (11)
Wyvern Primary School, Leicester

Love

Love is pink.
Love tastes like sweet strawberry milkshake.
Love smells like pure roses.
Love looks like two hearts together.
Love sounds like a heart thumping, *boom, boom!*
Love feels like a good kiss!

Hiren Ladha (9)
Wyvern Primary School, Leicester

The Lazy Lion

The lion has a golden mane
Under its clever brain.
He lies around and roars
And lets the lioness do the chores.
He watches TV all day long
Acting like a ping-pong ball.
The lioness was having a cub
But the lion was having a rub in the tub.
The lioness can't do any chores
But she had to make laws.
The lion wasn't happy
Because he had to change the nappy.

Aatish Chamunda (8)
Wyvern Primary School, Leicester

The Maze

My maze is tricky, you have to be clever
You can get trapped, so watch out
It will give you revenge
The ferocious walls will scare you to death
If you defeat my maze, you will be sorry
You might be exhausted but I don't care
So never try and come here because
If you are not very strong you can't go
Be careful now, listen to me
It is close to your house, please look for it
Because you can't defeat this maze
Be careful where you step!

Dilon Tanna (8)
Wyvern Primary School, Leicester

Promise And Manners

Before you make a promise you should think and keep it.
You should never make a fake promise.
You should never break a promise unless you're told to.
To show good manners you have to be helpful,
Listen to the person you're talking to,
Be kind and show good respect.

Hemisha Natu (7)

Wyvern Primary School, Leicester

Butterfly Poem

Butterfly, butterfly, fly in the sky
Butterfly, butterfly, flies so high
Butterfly, butterfly, lands on my thigh
Butterfly, butterfly, motionlessly lies
Butterfly, butterfly, gracefully dies.

Farheen Mulla (8)

Wyvern Primary School, Leicester

Young Writers Information

We hope you have enjoyed reading this book - and that you will continue to enjoy it in the coming years.

If you like reading and writing poetry drop us a line, or give us a call, and we'll send you a free information pack.

Alternatively if you would like to order further copies of this book or any of our other titles, then please give us a call or log onto our website at www.youngwriters.co.uk

Young Writers Information
Remus House
Coltsfoot Drive
Peterborough
PE2 9JX
(01733) 890066